Praying God's Promises

Developed and edited by Dorrie Philbeck

Design by Dana Krinsky

With heartfelt gratitude, I dedicate this intercessory prayer guide to my beloved daughter, Dana Krinsky. This prayer guide was actually her idea as a companion book to, *Prayer and Promises: 52 Inspirational Messages on Claiming God's Promises*. Her determination and invaluable help and support were essential in bringing this book to life.

I am also deeply thankful to those who generously took the time to review this book. Their guidance and advice were vital in making this book more engaging.

Copywrites

Table of Contents

Introduction

It was the mid-1980s when I attended the Wewoka Woods Campmeeting in Oklahoma with some friends. We were gathered in a tent listening to people share their testimonies. Someone shared their prayer experience and I wondered, "How can these people pray for an hour? What can they possibly talk to God about for all that time?" I could barely manage ten minutes of prayer myself. That week, they began sharing more with us about the power of claiming the promises of God. I started reading the Bible with renewed interest and discovering promises to claim for my children and myself. I had just begun my Christian journey a few years before and had many struggles trying to navigate the Christian life. I needed guidance. I found that claiming God's promises gave me a newfound success. Now, instead of trusting in myself, I knew how to put my trust in the Lord. After all, He pities my weakness and knows that I am made from the dust. Psalm 103:13,14. I can admit to God that I am powerless on my own and need His help in following His Word. As I began trusting in His promises and believing that God is faithful to His word, I finally started experiencing true victory over self and a deepening relationship with my Lord and Savior.

This book begins with practical guidance to help you deepen your prayer life and confidently trust in God's promises. The intercessory prayer pages are designed to assist you in thoughtfully composing and organizing prayers that are grounded in the promises of God's Word. Throughout, you'll also find encouraging quotes and insights designed to strengthen your faith in God's promises. As you explore these pages, you'll discover the support and tools needed to enrich your relationship with God and embrace His promises with renewed confidence and assurance.

In my quest to pray more effectively and intimately, I found the writings of Ellen G. White to be a constant inspiration and help. Her unwavering faith in the promises strengthens my own faith. It is my desire to share with you what I have learned from this humble, consecrated servant of the Lord.

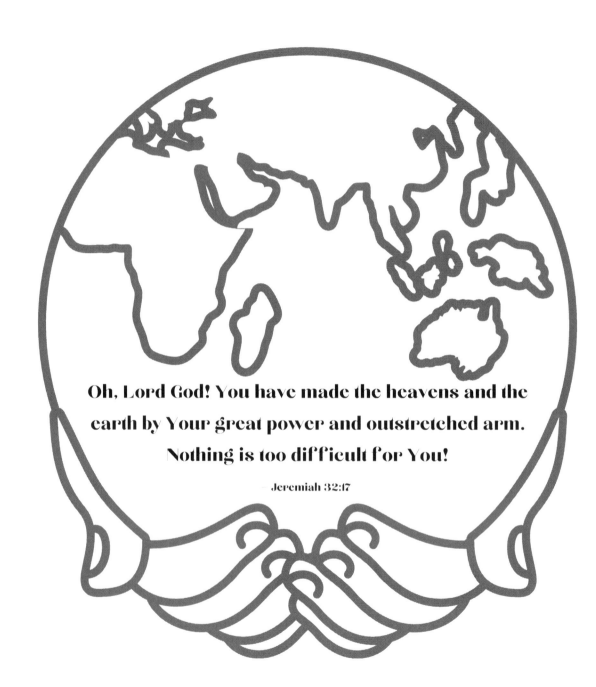

Oh, Lord God! You have made the heavens and the earth by Your great power and outstretched arm. Nothing is too difficult for You!

– Jeremiah 32:17

Praying and Claiming God's Promises

From the book, Thoughts from the Mount of Blessing, p.133

1) Every promise in the word of God furnishes us with subject matter for prayer presenting the pledged word of Jehovah as our assurance.

2) Whatever spiritual blessing we need, it is our privilege to claim it through Jesus. We may tell the Lord, with the simplicity of a child, exactly what we need.

3) We may state to Him our temporal matters, asking Him for bread and raiment as well as for the bread of life and the robe of Christ's righteousness. Your heavenly Father knows that you have need of all these things, and you are invited to ask Him concerning them.

4) It is through the name of Jesus that every favor is received. God will honor that name, and will supply your necessities from the riches of His liberality.

5) Do not forget that in coming to God as a father you acknowledge your relation to Him as a child. You not only trust His goodness, but in all things yield to His will, knowing that His love is changeless. You give yourself to do His work.

6) Take God's promises as your own, plead them before Him as His own words, and you will receive fullness of joy.

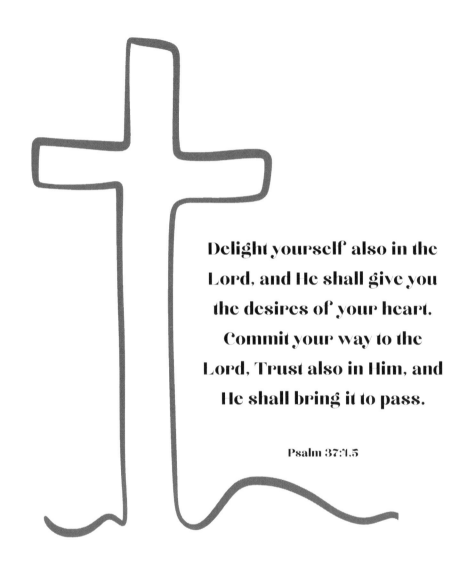

Delight yourself also in the Lord, and He shall give you the desires of your heart. Commit your way to the Lord, Trust also in Him, and He shall bring it to pass.

Psalm 37:4,5

Conditions to Answered Prayer

From the chapter in Steps to Christ, "The Privilege of Prayer," p.93-103

Prayer is the opening of the heart to God as to a friend. Not that it is necessary in order to make known to God what we are, but in order to enable us to receive Him. Prayer does not bring God down to us, but brings us up to Him.

There are certain conditions which we may expect that God will hear and answer our prayers.

- **Feel Your Need**
- **Trusting Faith**
- **Believe His Promises**
- **Forgiveness**
- **Persevering In Prayer**
- **Open Up Your Heart**
- **In Jesus Name**
- **Thankful Praise**

FEEL YOUR NEED
One of the first of these [conditions] is that we feel our need of help from Him.

Our great need is itself an argument and pleads most eloquently in our behalf. But the Lord is to be sought unto to do these things for us. He says, "Ask, and it shall be given you." *Matthew 7:7.*

Our heavenly Father waits to bestow upon us the fullness of His blessing. It is our privilege to drink largely at the fountain of boundless love. What a wonder it is that we pray so little! God is ready and willing to hear the sincere prayer of the humblest of His children, and yet there is much manifest reluctance on our part to make known our wants to God.

TRUSTING FAITH

Another element of prevailing prayer is faith. "He that cometh to God must believe that He is, and that He is a rewarder of them that diligently seek Him." *Hebrews 11:6*. Jesus said to His disciples, "What things soever ye desire, when ye pray, believe that ye receive them, and ye shall have them." *Mark 11:24*. Do we take Him at His word?

If we take counsel with our doubts and fears, or try to solve everything that we cannot see clearly, before we have faith, perplexities will only increase and deepen. But if we come to God, feeling helpless and dependent, as we really are, and in humble, trusting faith make known our wants to Him whose knowledge is infinite, who sees everything in creation, and who governs everything by His will and word, He can and will attend to our cry, and will let light shine into our hearts. Through sincere prayer we are brought into connection with the mind of the Infinite.

BELIEVE HIS PROMISES

He is faithful who has promised. When we do not receive the very things we asked for, at the time we ask, we are still to believe that the Lord hears and that He will answer our prayers. We are so erring and short-sighted that we sometimes ask for things that would not be a blessing to us, and our heavenly Father in love answers our prayers by giving us that which will be for our highest good—that which we ourselves would desire if with vision divinely enlightened we could see all things as they really are.

When our prayers seem not to be answered, we are to cling to the promise; for the time of answering will surely come, and we shall receive the blessing we need most... Rely upon His sure promise, "Ask, and it shall be given you."

FORGIVENESS

If we regard iniquity in our hearts, if we cling to any known sin, the Lord will not hear us; but the prayer of the penitent, contrite soul is always accepted. When all known wrongs are righted, we may believe that God will answer our petitions. Our own merit will never commend us to the favor of God; it is the worthiness of Jesus that will save us.

When we come to ask mercy and blessing from God we should have a spirit of love and forgiveness in our own hearts. How can we pray, "Forgive us our debts, as we forgive our debtors," and yet indulge an unforgiving spirit? *Matthew 6:12.* If we expect our own prayers to be heard we must forgive others in the same manner and to the same extent as we hope to be forgiven.

PERSEVERING IN PRAYER

Perseverance in prayer has been made a condition of receiving. We must pray always if we would grow in faith and experience. We are to... "continue in prayer, and watch in the same with thanksgiving." *Colossians 4:2...* Unceasing prayer is the unbroken union of the soul with God, so that life from God flows into our life; and from our life, purity and holiness flow back to God.

Make every effort to keep open the communion between Jesus and your own soul. Seek every opportunity to go where prayer is wont to be made. Those who are really seeking for communion with God will be seen in the prayer meeting, faithful to do their duty and earnest and anxious to reap all the benefits they can gain.

OPEN UP YOUR HEART

We should have the door of the heart open continually and our invitation going up that Jesus may come and abide as a heavenly guest in the soul.

We may close every door to impure imaginings and unholy thoughts by lifting the soul into the presence of God through sincere prayer. Those whose hearts are open to receive the support and blessing of God will walk in a holier atmosphere than that of earth and will have constant communion with heaven.

The beauty of holiness is to fill the hearts of God's children; and that this may be accomplished, we should seek for divine disclosures of heavenly things.

IN JESUS NAME

Jesus said, "Ye shall ask in My name, ... I will pray the Father for you: for the Father Himself loveth you." "I have chosen you: ... that whatsoever ye shall ask of the Father in My name, He may give it you." *John 16:26, 27; 15:16.*

But to pray in the name of Jesus is something more than a mere mention of that name at the beginning and the ending of a prayer. It is to pray in the mind and spirit of Jesus, while we believe His promises, rely upon His grace, and work His works.

THANKFUL PRAISE

We need to praise God more "for His goodness, and for His wonderful works to the children of men." *Psalm 107:8.* Our devotional exercises should not consist wholly in asking and receiving. Let us not be always thinking of our wants and never of the benefits we receive. We do not pray any too much, but we are too sparing of giving thanks.

If Christians would associate together, speaking to each other of the love of God and of the precious truths of redemption, their own hearts would be refreshed and they would refresh one another. We may be daily learning more of our heavenly Father, gaining a fresh experience of His grace; then we shall desire to speak of His love; and as we do this, our own hearts will be warmed and encouraged. If we thought and talked more of Jesus, and less of self, we should have far more of His presence.

Prayer of F.A.I.T.H.

Staying focused during prayer and knowing what to pray about can be challenging. Remember, there's no wrong way to pray—prayer is about opening your heart to God and connecting with Him. To help guide you in structuring your prayers, consider using the F.A.I.T.H. acronym.

Forgiveness

Come before God in humble confession to
receive both His forgiveness and cleansing.

(See Psalm 51:1-2; Ezekiel 36:25-27; 2 Cor. 7:10; Titus 2:14; 1 John 1:9)

Abide

Take time to abide in the presence of Jesus, looking to Him as your personal Savior. Read His Word as if He were speaking directly to you.

(See Matthew 28:20; John 8:31; John 14:23; John 15:7; 2 Cor. 6:16)

Intercession

Intercede in prayer for others, asking that they may be
strengthened with all power according to His divine promises.

(See Romans 1:8-9; 1 Cor. 1:4-8; Ephesians 1:16-20; Col. 1:9-11; 1 Tim. 2:1-6; 2 Thes. 1:11-12)

Thanksgiving & Praise

Give thanks to the Lord for His goodness and mercy; praise
Him openly, lifting your voice in gratitude and praise.

(See Psalm Psalm 103: 1-5; 107:8-9,31-32; Ephes. 5:19-20; Heb. 13:15)

Hope

Do not let your hope waver for
He who promised is faithful!

(See Romans 5:4; Romans 15:13; 1 Thess. 5:24; Hebrews 9:14; Hebrews 10:23)

Personalizing Promises

**She laid her finger upon the texts,
presenting before God His own words.**
— *Testimonies for the Church Volume 5, p.322*

Experience greater power in prayer by embracing God's promises as your own and presenting them as His own words. When you personalize His promises they will come alive as if He is speaking directly to you. Build a faith that rests in the promises of God for yourself and your loved ones by inserting a name (and/or an appropriate pronoun) in the blanks below.

Example — Call upon Me in the day of trouble; I will deliver *Name/Names* and *he/she/they* will honor Me.   — Psalm 50:15

I will bring the blind by a way they did not know; I will lead them in paths they have not known. I will make darkness light before them, and crooked places straight. These things I will do for _____, and not forsake _____.   — Isaiah 42:16

For I know the plans I have for _____, declares the Lord, plans to prosper _____ and not to harm _____, to give _____ a future and a hope.   — Jeremiah 29:11

Now may the God of hope fill _____ with all joy and peace as _____ believes in Him, so that _____ may overflow with hope by the power of the Holy Spirit.   — Romans 15:13

Now thanks be to God who always leads _____ in triumph in Christ, and through _____ diffuses the fragrance of His knowledge in every place.   — 2 Corinthians 2:14

The promises of God can be repeated over and over again and with every repetition light comes to the mind.
— *The Gospel Herald, July 1, 1900*

I ask that out of the riches of His glory He may strengthen _____

with power through His Spirit in _____ inner being,

— Ephesians 3:16

Being confident of this, that He who began a good work in _____

will carry it on to completion until the day of Christ Jesus.

— Philippians 1:6

For this reason, since the day we heard about _____, we have

not stopped praying for _____ and asking God to fill

_____ with the knowledge of His will in all spiritual wisdom

and understanding, so that _____ may walk in a manner

worthy of the Lord and may please Him in every way: bearing fruit in every

good work, growing in the knowledge of God, — Colossians 1:9,10

He has rescued _____ from the dominion of darkness and

brought _____ into the kingdom of His beloved Son, in whom

_____ has redemption, the forgiveness of sins.

— Colossians 1:13,14

Now may the God of peace Himself sanctify _____

completely, and may _____ entire spirit, soul, and body be

kept blameless at the coming of our Lord Jesus Christ. The One who calls

_____ is faithful, and He will do it.

— 1 Thessalonians 5:23,24

And the Lord will deliver _____ from every evil work and

preserve _____ for His heavenly kingdom. To Him be glory

forever and ever. Amen! — 2 Timothy 4:7

Let us then approach the throne of grace with confidence, so that we may receive mercy and find grace to help us in our time of need.

Hebrews 4:16

Intercessory Prayer Pages

The prayer pages in this section are more than just a prayer list or a prayer journal; they are a tool to help you organize and thoughtfully write out your intercessory prayers based on God's promises. Whether you're a seasoned prayer warrior or new to prayer, these Intercessory Prayer Pages are designed to support you in praying specific petitions.

Each Intercessory Prayer Page is divided into four sections:

What is the need?: This section is the focus of your intercession. Whether you're praying for a loved one, a church project, or life challenges, there's a place to check a category for your prayer, allowing you to organize and pray for a different category each day of the week if you choose to do so.

Bible Promise: The foundation of effective prayer lies in claiming God's promises. The word of God holds immense power. "The same power that Christ exercised when He walked visibly among men is in His word. It was by His word that Jesus healed disease and cast out demons; by His word He stilled the sea and raised the dead, and the people bore witness that His word was with power." — *The Ministry of Healing, p.122*

You can find powerful promises to claim starting on page 121. There are many books available that offer Bible promises arranged by topic. Better yet, as you read the Bible you may note your own favorite promises in the place provided on page 135.

Write your prayer using the Bible promise: You may find the prayer acronym F.A.I.T.H. on page 11 helpful as you write out your prayer. Pray with confidence by inviting the Holy Spirit to guide your petitions. His divine insight will reveal what you should ask for. "The prayer which God accepts is the simple, earnest petition from a soul that feels its need; and He promised to send the Holy Spirit to indite their prayers." — *The Review and Herald, February 9, 1897*

Request Updates / Answer: Record updates and changes to your requests here, and note when your prayers are answered.

Faith plants itself on the promises of God, and claims them as surety that He will do just as He said He would. Jesus comes to the sinful, helpless, needy soul, and says, "What things soever ye desire, when ye pray, believe that ye receive them, and ye shall have them." Believe; claim the promises, and praise God that you do receive the things you have asked of Him, and when your need is greatest, you will experience His blessing and receive special help.

—Signs of the Times, May 22, 1884

What is the need?

Bible Promise
See Promises to Claim pages: 121-133

Praying for:

- [ ] Self
- [ ] Family
- [ ] Friend
- [ ] Church
- [ ] Ministry
- [ ] Life Issues

Write your prayer using the Bible promise. Claim it again & again!
Invite the Holy Spirit to guide you as you write out your prayer.

Date:

Request Updates / Answer

Date:

Date:

Date:

It is not our efforts that
bring victory; it is seeing God
behind the promise, and
believing and trusting Him.
Grasp by faith the hand of
infinite power. The Lord is
faithful who has promised.

— The Review and Herald, December 29, 1910

What is the need?

_____

_____

_____

_____

Bible Promise
See Promises to Claim pages: 121-133

_____

_____

_____

_____

_____

_____

_____

Praying for:

☐ Self   ☐ Church

☐ Family   ☐ Ministry

☐ Friend   ☐ Life Issues

Write your prayer using the Bible promise. Claim it again & again!
Invite the Holy Spirit to guide you as you write out your prayer.

_____

_____

_____

_____

_____

_____

_____

_____

_____

_____

Date:

Request Updates / Answer

Date:

Date:

Date:

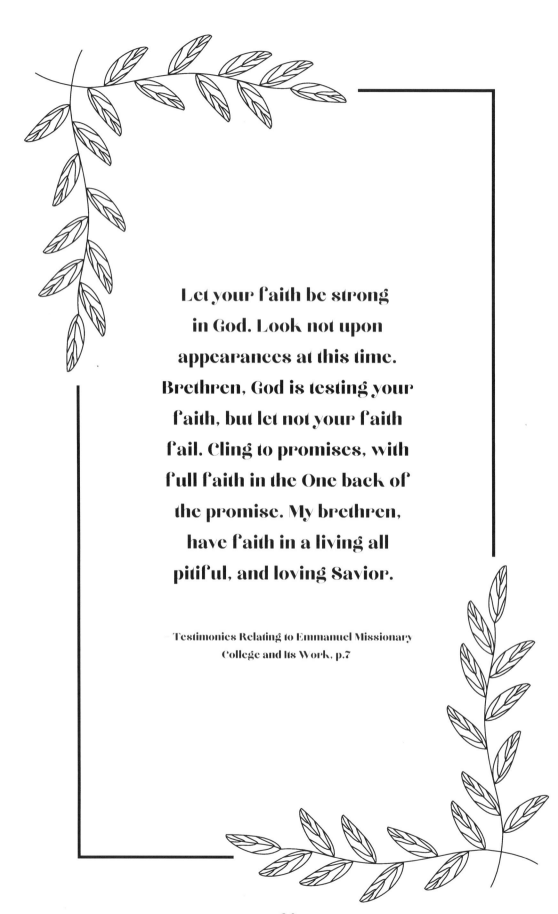

Let your faith be strong in God. Look not upon appearances at this time. Brethren, God is testing your faith, but let not your faith fail. Cling to promises, with full faith in the One back of the promise. My brethren, have faith in a living all pitiful, and loving Savior.

Testimonies Relating to Emmanuel Missionary College and Its Work, p.7

What is the need?

Bible Promise

See Promises to Claim pages: 121-133

Praying for:

- ☐ Self
- ☐ Family
- ☐ Friend
- ☐ Church
- ☐ Ministry
- ☐ Life Issues

Write your prayer using the Bible promise. Claim it again & again!

Invite the Holy Spirit to guide you as you write out your prayer.

Date:

Request Updates / Answer

Date:

Date:

Date:

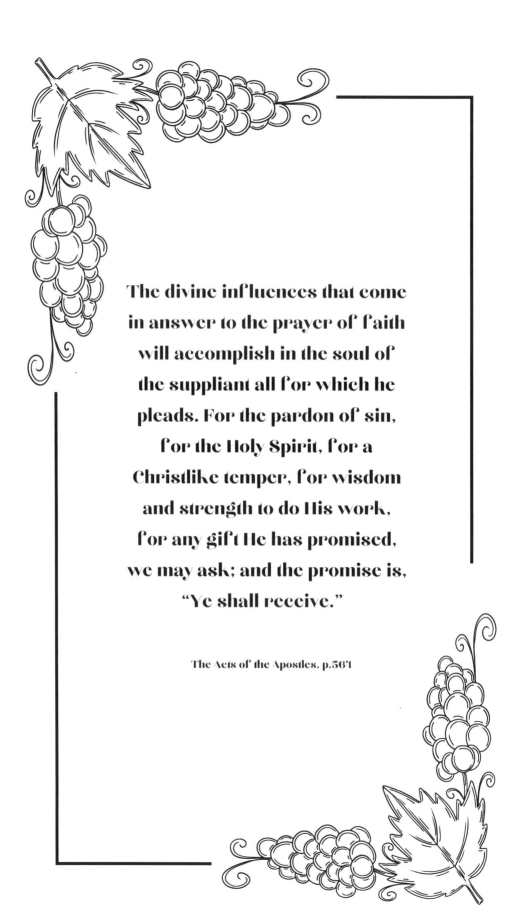

The divine influences that come in answer to the prayer of faith will accomplish in the soul of the suppliant all for which he pleads. For the pardon of sin, for the Holy Spirit, for a Christlike temper, for wisdom and strength to do His work, for any gift He has promised, we may ask; and the promise is, "Ye shall receive."

The Acts of the Apostles, p.564

What is the need?

_____

_____

_____

_____

Bible Promise
See Promises to Claim pages: 121-133

_____

_____

_____

_____

_____

_____

_____

_____

Praying for:

☐ Self ☐ Church

☐ Family ☐ Ministry

☐ Friend ☐ Life Issues

Write your prayer using the Bible promise. Claim it again & again!
Invite the Holy Spirit to guide you as you write out your prayer.

_____

_____

_____

_____

_____

_____

_____

_____

_____

_____

Date:

Request Updates / Answer

Date:

Date:

Date:

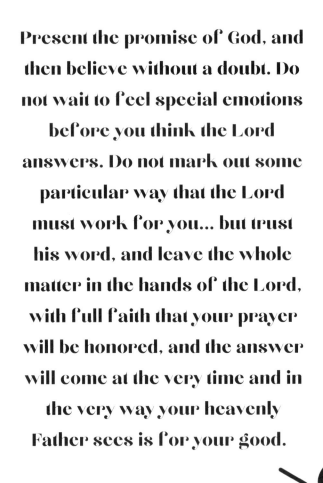

Present the promise of God, and then believe without a doubt. Do not wait to feel special emotions before you think the Lord answers. Do not mark out some particular way that the Lord must work for you... but trust his word, and leave the whole matter in the hands of the Lord, with full faith that your prayer will be honored, and the answer will come at the very time and in the very way your heavenly Father sees is for your good.

Sabbath School Worker, April 1, 1886

What is the need?

_____
_____
_____
_____

Praying for:

☐ Self   ☐ Church
☐ Family   ☐ Ministry
☐ Friend   ☐ Life Issues

Bible Promise
See Promises to Claim pages: 121-133

_____
_____
_____
_____
_____
_____
_____

Write your prayer using the Bible promise. Claim it again & again!
Invite the Holy Spirit to guide you as you write out your prayer.

_____
_____
_____
_____
_____
_____
_____
_____
_____
_____
_____

Date:

Request Updates / Answer

Date: _____
Date: _____
Date:

Faith is a very simple matter; it is confidence in God... If, in a humble, trustful spirit, you ask for the things he has promised, you will receive, because the word of God is pledged: "Ye shall receive." Keep praying, keep believing, keep looking unto Jesus, and watching unto prayer. You are to live your faith in the Lord, saying, "I do believe I receive the things I ask of him."

The Youth's Instructor, August 30, 1894

What is the need?

Bible Promise
See Promises to Claim pages: 121-133

Praying for:

- [ ] Self
- [ ] Family
- [ ] Friend
- [ ] Church
- [ ] Ministry
- [ ] Life Issues

Write your prayer using the Bible promise. Claim it again & again!
Invite the Holy Spirit to guide you as you write out your prayer.

Date:

Request Updates / Answer

Date:

Date:

Date:

We are to come before the mercy-seat with reverence, calling up to our mind the promises that God has given, contemplating the goodness of God, and offering up thankful praises for his unchangeable love. We are not to trust in our finite prayers, but in the word of our Heavenly Father, in his assurance of his love for us.

The Review and Herald, November 19, 1895

What is the need?

Bible Promise
See Promises to Claim pages: 121-133

Praying for:

- [ ] Self
- [ ] Family
- [ ] Friend
- [ ] Church
- [ ] Ministry
- [ ] Life Issues

Write your prayer using the Bible promise. Claim it again & again!
Invite the Holy Spirit to guide you as you write out your prayer.

Date:

Request Updates / Answer

Date:

Date:

Date:

If you ask in faith [for the deep moving of the Holy Spirit upon hearts], presenting the name of God's Son as your endorsement, your prayer will be heard and answered. God's goodness makes this promise unchangeable. The infallibility of the promise is to inspire faith in the one who asks. "Ask, and ye shall receive."

Signs of the Times, August 7, 1901

What is the need?

Bible Promise
See Promises to Claim pages: 121-133

Praying for:

- ☐ Self
- ☐ Family
- ☐ Friend
- ☐ Church
- ☐ Ministry
- ☐ Life Issues

Write your prayer using the Bible promise. Claim it again & again!
Invite the Holy Spirit to guide you as you write out your prayer.

Date:

Request Updates / Answer

Date:

Date:

Date:

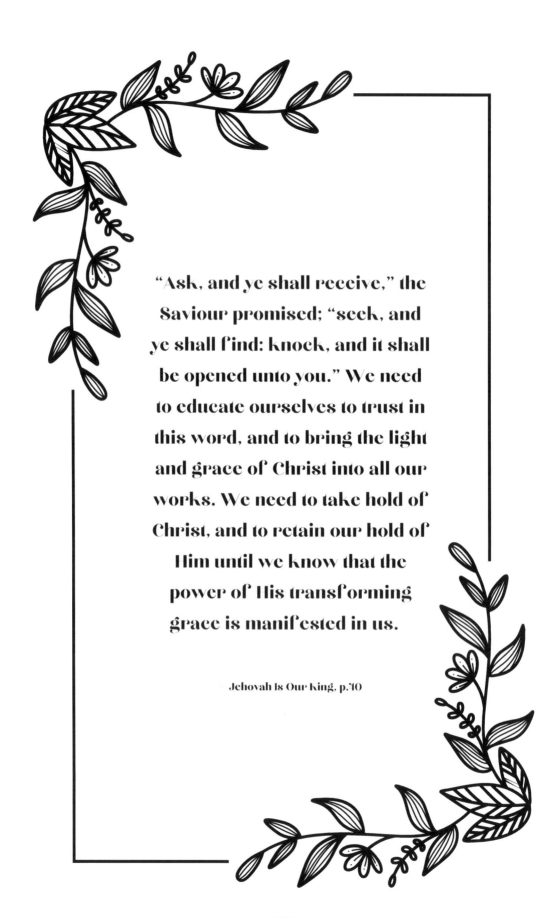

"Ask, and ye shall receive," the Saviour promised; "seek, and ye shall find: knock, and it shall be opened unto you." We need to educate ourselves to trust in this word, and to bring the light and grace of Christ into all our works. We need to take hold of Christ, and to retain our hold of Him until we know that the power of His transforming grace is manifested in us.

Jehovah Is Our King, p.70

What is the need?

_____
_____
_____
_____

Praying for:

☐ Self   ☐ Church
☐ Family   ☐ Ministry
☐ Friend   ☐ Life Issues

Bible Promise

See Promises to Claim pages: 121-133

_____
_____
_____
_____
_____
_____
_____
_____

Write your prayer using the Bible promise. Claim it again & again!

Invite the Holy Spirit to guide you as you write out your prayer.

_____
_____
_____
_____
_____
_____
_____
_____
_____
_____

Date:

Request Updates / Answer

Date: _____
Date: _____
Date: _____

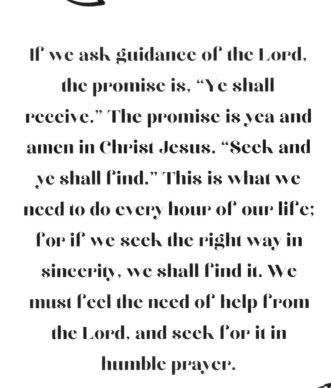

If we ask guidance of the Lord, the promise is, "Ye shall receive." The promise is yea and amen in Christ Jesus. "Seek and ye shall find." This is what we need to do every hour of our life; for if we seek the right way in sincerity, we shall find it. We must feel the need of help from the Lord, and seek for it in humble prayer.

Signs of the Times, August 15, 1892

34

What is the need?

Bible Promise
See Promises to Claim pages: 121-133

Praying for:

☐ Self   ☐ Church
☐ Family   ☐ Ministry
☐ Friend   ☐ Life Issues

Write your prayer using the Bible promise. Claim it again & again!
Invite the Holy Spirit to guide you as you write out your prayer.

Date:

Request Updates / Answer

Date:

Date:

Date:

What a privilege it is that we may draw near to him by faith, presenting the promises given in his word. Let us encourage and refresh our souls with these sure promises, pleading our great need as the reason why they should be fulfilled. Let us learn the simple art of faith.

Signs of the Times, March 5, 1885

What is the need?

Bible Promise
See Promises to Claim pages: 121-133

Praying for:

☐ Self   ☐ Church

☐ Family   ☐ Ministry

☐ Friend   ☐ Life Issues

Write your prayer using the Bible promise. Claim it again & again!
Invite the Holy Spirit to guide you as you write out your prayer.

Date:

Request Updates / Answer

Date:

Date:

Date:

Difficulties may appear in our way... Perhaps they will not appear at all, because the Lord is hearing and answering prayer. We need to pray much more than we do. We need to bring the promises of the Lord to Him, and thank and praise Him for what He has promised to give us if we will follow on to know Him.

Record of Progress and An Appeal In Behalf of the Boulder Colorado Sanitarium, p.39

What is the need?

Bible Promise
See Promises to Claim pages: 121–133

Praying for:

- ☐ Self
- ☐ Family
- ☐ Friend
- ☐ Church
- ☐ Ministry
- ☐ Life Issues

Write your prayer using the Bible promise. Claim it again & again!
Invite the Holy Spirit to guide you as you write out your prayer.

Date:

Request Updates / Answer

Date:

Date:

Date:

Not because we see or feel that God hears us are we to believe. We are to trust in His promises. When we come to Him in faith, every petition enters the heart of God. When we have asked for His blessing, we should believe that we receive it, and thank Him that we have received it. Then we are to go about our duties, assured that the blessing will be realized when we need it most. When we have learned to do this, we shall know that our prayers are answered. God will do for us "exceeding abundantly," "according to the riches of His glory," and "the working of His mighty power."

— The Desire of Ages, p.200

What is the need?

Bible Promise
See Promises to Claim pages: 121-133

Praying for:

- [ ] Self
- [ ] Family
- [ ] Friend
- [ ] Church
- [ ] Ministry
- [ ] Life Issues

Write your prayer using the Bible promise. Claim it again & again!
Invite the Holy Spirit to guide you as you write out your prayer.

Date:

Request Updates / Answer

Date:

Date:

Date:

Every promise in the Word of God is for us. In your prayers, present the pledged word of Jehovah, and by faith claim His promises. His word is the assurance that if you ask in faith, you will receive all spiritual blessings. Continue to ask, and you will receive exceeding abundantly above all that you ask or think. Educate yourself to have unlimited confidence in God. Cast all your care upon Him. Wait patiently for Him, and He will bring it to pass.

Signs of the Times, November 18, 1903

What is the need?

_____

_____

_____

_____

Bible Promise
See Promises to Claim pages: 121-133

_____

_____

_____

_____

_____

_____

_____

_____

Praying for:

☐ Self   ☐ Church

☐ Family   ☐ Ministry

☐ Friend   ☐ Life Issues

Write your prayer using the Bible promise. Claim it again & again!
Invite the Holy Spirit to guide you as you write out your prayer.

_____

_____

_____

_____

_____

_____

_____

_____

_____

_____

Date:

Request Updates / Answer

Date: _____

Date: _____

Date: _____

The most precious promises of God are to be claimed, and held fast, by the exercise of faith... Take God's promises as your own, plead them before him as his own words; and you will receive fullness of joy.

The Review and Herald, September 11, 1888

What is the need?

Bible Promise
See Promises to Claim pages: 121-133

Praying for:

☐ Self   ☐ Church

☐ Family   ☐ Ministry

☐ Friend   ☐ Life Issues

Write your prayer using the Bible promise. Claim it again & again!
Invite the Holy Spirit to guide you as you write out your prayer.

Date:

Request Updates / Answer

Date:

Date:

Date:

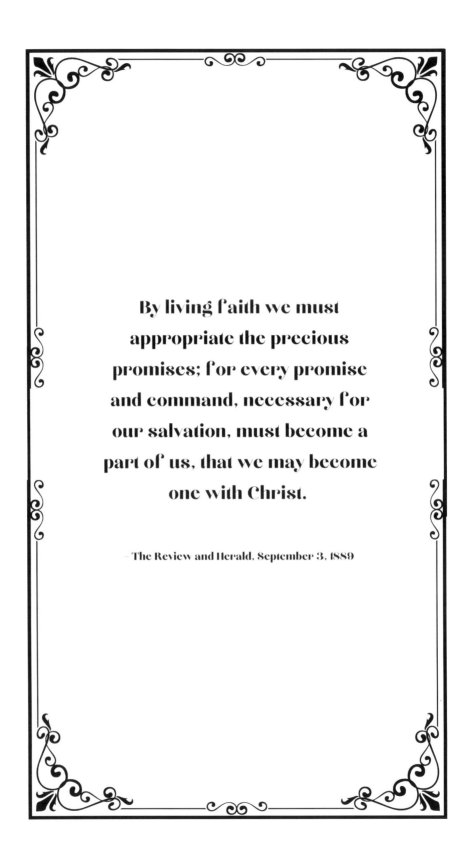

By living faith we must appropriate the precious promises; for every promise and command, necessary for our salvation, must become a part of us, that we may become one with Christ.

– The Review and Herald, September 3, 1889

What is the need?

Bible Promise
See Promises to Claim pages: 121-133

Praying for:

☐ Self   ☐ Church
☐ Family   ☐ Ministry
☐ Friend   ☐ Life Issues

Write your prayer using the Bible promise. Claim it again & again!
Invite the Holy Spirit to guide you as you write out your prayer.

Date:

Request Updates / Answer

Date:

Date:

Date:

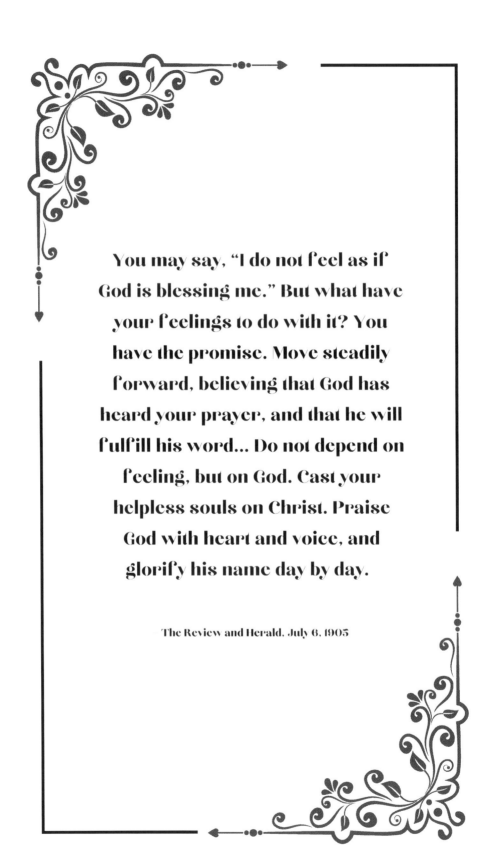

You may say, "I do not feel as if God is blessing me." But what have your feelings to do with it? You have the promise. Move steadily forward, believing that God has heard your prayer, and that he will fulfill his word... Do not depend on feeling, but on God. Cast your helpless souls on Christ. Praise God with heart and voice, and glorify his name day by day.

The Review and Herald, July 6, 1905

What is the need?

Bible Promise

See Promises to Claim pages: 121-133

Praying for:

- ☐ Self
- ☐ Family
- ☐ Friend
- ☐ Church
- ☐ Ministry
- ☐ Life Issues

Write your prayer using the Bible promise. Claim it again & again!

Invite the Holy Spirit to guide you as you write out your prayer.

Date:

Request Updates / Answer

Date:

Date:

Date:

The faith that recognizes Christ
leads the soul to rest implicitly
upon the promises, because God
is behind them. There is hope
for the most desponding. Those
who take Christ at his word, who
surrender their souls to his
keeping, their lives to his
ordering, will find peace,
quietude, and rest. He will impart
grace to the needy soul.

Signs of the Times, May 28, 1896

What is the need?

_____

_____

_____

_____

Praying for:

☐ Self ☐ Church

☐ Family ☐ Ministry

☐ Friend ☐ Life Issues

Bible Promise
See Promises to Claim pages: 121-133

_____

_____

_____

_____

_____

_____

_____

_____

Write your prayer using the Bible promise. Claim it again & again!
Invite the Holy Spirit to guide you as you write out your prayer.

_____

_____

_____

_____

_____

_____

_____

_____

_____

_____

Date:

Request Updates / Answer

Date: _____

Date: _____

Date:

The Christian whose heart is thus stayed upon God cannot be overcome. No evil arts can destroy his peace. All the promises of God's word, all the power of divine grace, all the resources of Jehovah, are pledged to secure his deliverance.

Gospel Workers, p.254

What is the need?

Bible Promise
See Promises to Claim pages: 121-133

Praying for:

- ☐ Self
- ☐ Family
- ☐ Friend
- ☐ Church
- ☐ Ministry
- ☐ Life Issues

Write your prayer using the Bible promise. Claim it again & again!
Invite the Holy Spirit to guide you as you write out your prayer.

Date:

Request Updates / Answer

Date:

Date:

Date:

Bow before God; open before the Lord your Bibles containing the divine promises; take your position upon them... The words and promises of God are the only foundation of our faith. Take the word of God as truth, as a living, speaking voice to you, and obey faithfully every requirement. God is faithful who hath promised.

Sabbath School Worker, April 1, 1886

What is the need?

Bible Promise
See Promises to Claim pages: 121-133

Praying for:

☐ Self   ☐ Church
☐ Family ☐ Ministry
☐ Friend ☐ Life Issues

Write your prayer using the Bible promise. Claim it again & again!
Invite the Holy Spirit to guide you as you write out your prayer.

Date:

Request Updates / Answer

Date:

Date:

Date:

Take time to pray, and as you pray, believe that God hears you. Have faith mixed with your prayers. You may not at all times feel the immediate answer; but then it is that faith is tried. You are proved to see whether you will trust in God, whether you have living, abiding faith. "Faithful is He that calleth you, who also will do it." Walk the narrow plank of faith. Trust all on the promises of the Lord.

— Testimonies for the Church Volume 1, p.167

What is the need?

Bible Promise

See Promises to Claim pages: 121-133

Praying for:

☐ Self   ☐ Church

☐ Family   ☐ Ministry

☐ Friend   ☐ Life Issues

Write your prayer using the Bible promise. Claim it again & again!

Invite the Holy Spirit to guide you as you write out your prayer.

Date:

Request Updates / Answer

Date:

Date:

Date:

If we walk in the light as Christ is in the light, we may come to the throne of grace with holy boldness. We may present the promises of God in living faith, and urge our petitions. Although we are weak, and erring, and unworthy, "the Spirit helpeth our infirmities."... When we have offered our petition once, we must not then abandon it, but say, as did Jacob when he wrestled all night with the angel, "I will not let thee go, except thou bless me," and like him we shall prevail.

Signs of the Times, May 15, 1884

What is the need?

Bible Promise
See Promises to Claim pages: 121-133

Praying for:

- ☐ Self
- ☐ Family
- ☐ Friend
- ☐ Church
- ☐ Ministry
- ☐ Life Issues

Write your prayer using the Bible promise. Claim it again & again!
Invite the Holy Spirit to guide you as you write out your prayer.

Date:

Request Updates / Answer

Date:

Date:

Date:

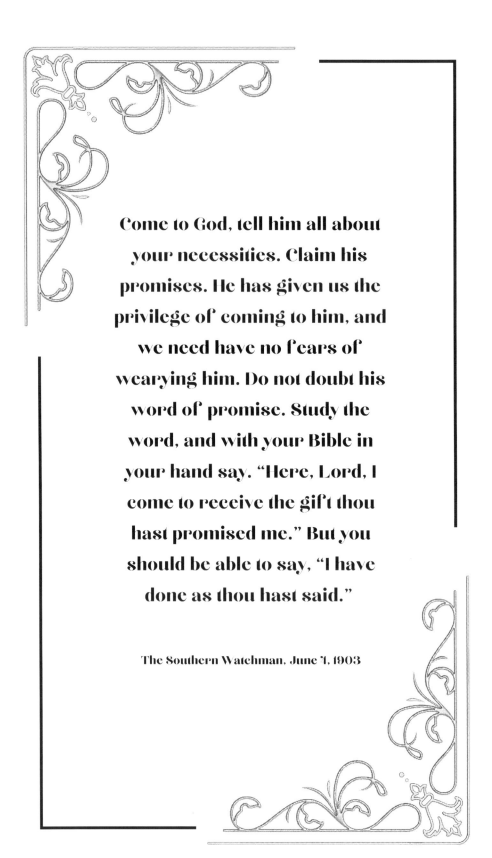

Come to God, tell him all about your necessities. Claim his promises. He has given us the privilege of coming to him, and we need have no fears of wearying him. Do not doubt his word of promise. Study the word, and with your Bible in your hand say. "Here, Lord, I come to receive the gift thou hast promised me." But you should be able to say, "I have done as thou hast said."

The Southern Watchman, June 4, 1903

What is the need?

_____
_____
_____
_____

Bible Promise

See Promises to Claim pages: 121-133

_____
_____
_____
_____
_____
_____
_____

Praying for:

- [ ] Self
- [ ] Family
- [ ] Friend
- [ ] Church
- [ ] Ministry
- [ ] Life Issues

Write your prayer using the Bible promise. Claim it again & again!

Invite the Holy Spirit to guide you as you write out your prayer.

_____
_____
_____
_____
_____
_____
_____
_____
_____
_____

Date:

Request Updates / Answer

Date: _____
Date: _____
Date:

Let our prayers ascend to God for his converting, transforming grace. Meetings should be held in every church for solemn prayer and earnest searching of the word to know what is truth. Take the promises of God, and ask God in living faith for the outpouring of his Holy Spirit. When the Holy Spirit is shed upon us, marrow and fatness will be drawn from the word of God.

The Review and Herald, February 25, 1890

What is the need?

Bible Promise
See Promises to Claim pages: 121-133

Praying for:

- [ ] Self
- [ ] Family
- [ ] Friend
- [ ] Church
- [ ] Ministry
- [ ] Life Issues

Write your prayer using the Bible promise. Claim it again & again!
Invite the Holy Spirit to guide you as you write out your prayer.

Date:

Request Updates / Answer

Date:

Date:

Date:

May God help us to gather up the jewels of his promises, and deck memory's hall with the gems of his word. We should be armed with the promises of God. Our souls should be barricaded with them.

— The Review and Herald, March 11, 1890

What is the need?

Bible Promise
See Promises to Claim pages: 121-133

Praying for:

- [ ] Self
- [ ] Family
- [ ] Friend
- [ ] Church
- [ ] Ministry
- [ ] Life Issues

Write your prayer using the Bible promise. Claim it again & again!
Invite the Holy Spirit to guide you as you write out your prayer.

Date:

Request Updates / Answer

Date:

Date:

Date:

When Satan comes in with his darkness, and seeks to fill my soul with gloom, I repeat some precious promise of God... As I do this, the light of the glory of God fills my soul. I will not look at the darkness.

— The Review and Herald, March 11, 1890

What is the need?

Bible Promise
See Promises to Claim pages: 121-133

Praying for:

☐ Self   ☐ Church
☐ Family   ☐ Ministry
☐ Friend   ☐ Life Issues

Write your prayer using the Bible promise. Claim it again & again!
Invite the Holy Spirit to guide you as you write out your prayer.

Date:

Request Updates / Answer

Date:

Date:

Date:

If you come with true contrition of soul, you need not feel that you are at all presumptuous in asking for what God has promised. Presumption is asking for things to gratify selfish inclination; for human enjoyment in earthly things. But when you ask for the spiritual blessings you so much need in order that you may perfect a character after Christ's likeness, the Lord assures you that you are asking according to a promise that will be verified. You cannot show greater honor to Jesus Christ and your heavenly Father than to believe the word of God.

The Youth's Instructor, August 23, 1894

What is the need?

Bible Promise
See Promises to Claim pages: 121-133

Praying for:

- [ ] Self
- [ ] Family
- [ ] Friend
- [ ] Church
- [ ] Ministry
- [ ] Life Issues

Write your prayer using the Bible promise. Claim it again & again!
Invite the Holy Spirit to guide you as you write out your prayer.

Date:

Request Updates / Answer

Date:

Date:

Date:

Talk of the mighty power of Christ to bless all who come unto him. Jesus lives. Move out by faith, and claim the promises of God... Wherever you are, however trying your circumstances, do not talk discouragement. The Bible is full of rich promises. Can you not believe them?

Historical Sketches, p.129

What is the need?

_____

Bible Promise

See Promises to Claim pages: 121-133

_____

Praying for:

☐ Self   ☐ Church

☐ Family   ☐ Ministry

☐ Friend   ☐ Life Issues

Write your prayer using the Bible promise. Claim it again & again!
Invite the Holy Spirit to guide you as you write out your prayer.

_____

Date:

Request Updates / Answer

Date: _____

Date: _____

Date:

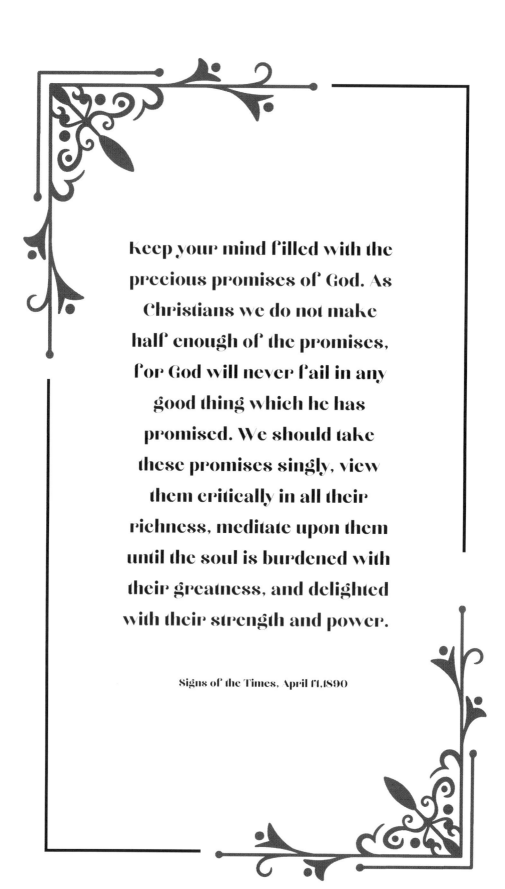

Keep your mind filled with the precious promises of God. As Christians we do not make half enough of the promises, for God will never fail in any good thing which he has promised. We should take these promises singly, view them critically in all their richness, meditate upon them until the soul is burdened with their greatness, and delighted with their strength and power.

Signs of the Times, April 14,1890

What is the need?

_____
_____
_____
_____
_____

Bible Promise
See Promises to Claim pages: 121-133

_____
_____
_____
_____
_____
_____
_____

Praying for:

☐ Self   ☐ Church

☐ Family   ☐ Ministry

☐ Friend   ☐ Life Issues

Write your prayer using the Bible promise. Claim it again & again!
Invite the Holy Spirit to guide you as you write out your prayer.

_____
_____
_____
_____
_____
_____
_____
_____
_____
_____

Date:

Request Updates / Answer

Date: _____

Date: _____

Date: _____

God's promise is given as much to children and youth as to those of more mature age. Whenever God has given a promise, let the children and youth turn it into a petition, and beg the Lord to do those things for them in their experience, that he did for Jesus, his only begotten Son, when in human necessity he looked to God, asking for the things which he needed.

The Youth's Instructor, August 23, 1894

What is the need?

_____
_____
_____
_____

Bible Promise
See Promises to Claim pages: 121-133

_____
_____
_____
_____
_____
_____
_____

Praying for:

☐ Self   ☐ Church

☐ Family   ☐ Ministry

☐ Friend   ☐ Life Issues

Write your prayer using the Bible promise. Claim it again & again!
Invite the Holy Spirit to guide you as you write out your prayer.

_____
_____
_____
_____
_____
_____
_____
_____
_____
_____

Date:

Request Updates / Answer

Date: _____

Date: _____

Date: _____

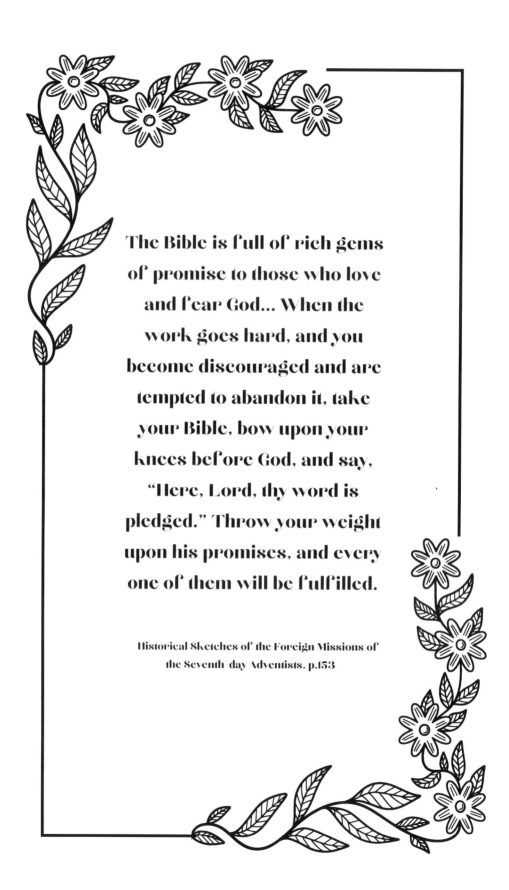

The Bible is full of rich gems of promise to those who love and fear God... When the work goes hard, and you become discouraged and are tempted to abandon it, take your Bible, bow upon your knees before God, and say, "Here, Lord, thy word is pledged." Throw your weight upon his promises, and every one of them will be fulfilled.

Historical Sketches of the Foreign Missions of the Seventh-day Adventists, p.153

What is the need?

Bible Promise
See Promises to Claim pages: 121-133

Praying for:

- ☐ Self
- ☐ Family
- ☐ Friend
- ☐ Church
- ☐ Ministry
- ☐ Life Issues

Write your prayer using the Bible promise. Claim it again & again!
Invite the Holy Spirit to guide you as you write out your prayer.

Date:

Request Updates / Answer

Date:

Date:

Date:

Pray in faith. "This is the victory that overcometh the world, even our faith." Prevailing prayer is the prayer of living faith; it takes God at his word, and claims his promises. Feeling has nothing to do with faith... How strange it is that men will put confidence in the word of their fellow-men, and yet find it so hard to exercise living faith in God! The promises are ample; why not accept them just as they read?

Signs of the Times, November 18, 1886

What is the need?

Bible Promise
See Promises to Claim pages: 121-133

Praying for:

- [ ] Self
- [ ] Family
- [ ] Friend
- [ ] Church
- [ ] Ministry
- [ ] Life Issues

Write your prayer using the Bible promise. Claim it again & again!
Invite the Holy Spirit to guide you as you write out your prayer.

Date:

Request Updates / Answer

Date:

Date:

Date:

Christ has promised the Holy Spirit to guide us into all truth and righteousness and holiness. The Spirit of God is not given by measure to those who earnestly seek for it, who by faith stand upon the promises of God. They plead the pledged word of God, saying, "Thou hast said it. I will take Thee at Thy word."

Signs of the Times, July 15, 1908

What is the need?

Bible Promise
See Promises to Claim pages: 121-133

Praying for:

- ☐ Self
- ☐ Family
- ☐ Friend
- ☐ Church
- ☐ Ministry
- ☐ Life Issues

Write your prayer using the Bible promise. Claim it again & again!
Invite the Holy Spirit to guide you as you write out your prayer.

Date:

Request Updates / Answer

Date:

Date:

Date:

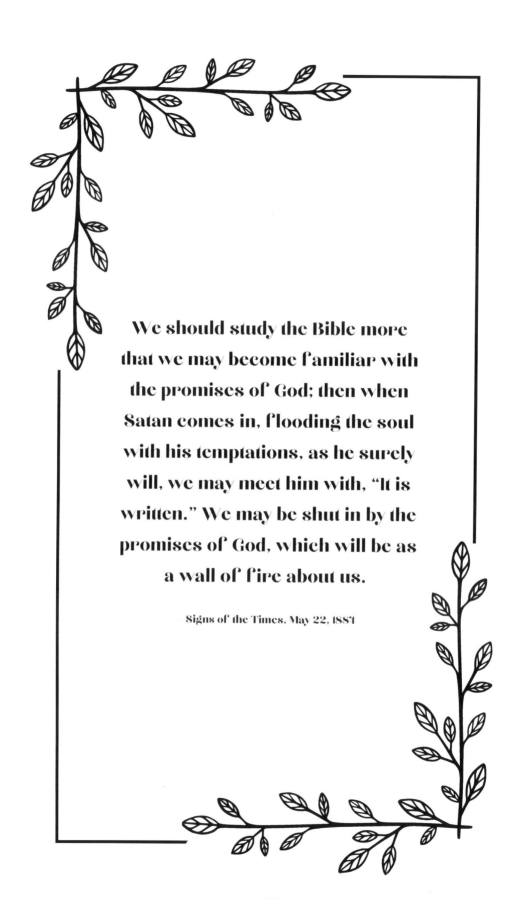

We should study the Bible more that we may become familiar with the promises of God; then when Satan comes in, flooding the soul with his temptations, as he surely will, we may meet him with, "It is written." We may be shut in by the promises of God, which will be as a wall of fire about us.

Signs of the Times, May 22, 1884

What is the need?

Bible Promise
See Promises to Claim pages: 121-133

Praying for:

- [ ] Self
- [ ] Family
- [ ] Friend
- [ ] Church
- [ ] Ministry
- [ ] Life Issues

Write your prayer using the Bible promise. Claim it again & again!
Invite the Holy Spirit to guide you as you write out your prayer.

Date:

Request Updates / Answer

Date:

Date:

Date:

The Bible is the voice of God to man... ask God for the aid of his Holy Spirit, who will teach us all things. Carefully study the Bible, verse by verse, praying that God will give you wisdom to understand his word. Take one verse, and concentrate your mind on it, praying to ascertain the thought God has put in that verse for you. Dwell upon the thought until it becomes your own, and you know "what saith the Lord."

The Review and Herald, August 4, 1896

What is the need?

Bible Promise
See Promises to Claim pages: 121-133

Praying for:

- ☐ Self
- ☐ Family
- ☐ Friend
- ☐ Church
- ☐ Ministry
- ☐ Life Issues

Write your prayer using the Bible promise. Claim it again & again!
Invite the Holy Spirit to guide you as you write out your prayer.

Date:

Request Updates / Answer

Date:

Date:

Date:

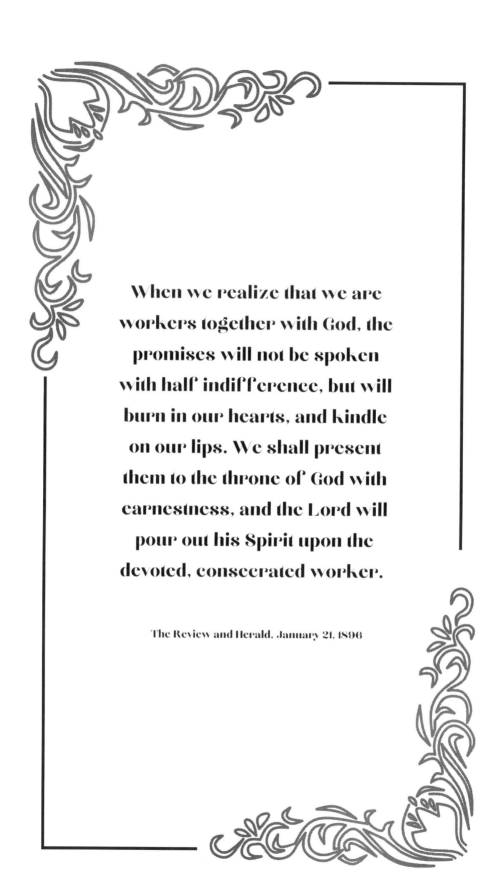

When we realize that we are workers together with God, the promises will not be spoken with half indifference, but will burn in our hearts, and kindle on our lips. We shall present them to the throne of God with earnestness, and the Lord will pour out his Spirit upon the devoted, consecrated worker.

The Review and Herald, January 21, 1896

What is the need?

_____

Bible Promise
See Promises to Claim pages: 121-133

_____

Praying for:

☐ Self   ☐ Church

☐ Family   ☐ Ministry

☐ Friend   ☐ Life Issues

Write your prayer using the Bible promise. Claim it again & again!
Invite the Holy Spirit to guide you as you write out your prayer.

_____

Date:

Request Updates / Answer

Date: _____

Date: _____

Date: _____

There is need of elevating our thoughts to dwell upon the promises of God. There is need of encouraging our faith and hope by exercise. Lay your soul before your heavenly Father in all its weakness and want, and repeat the assurances of his word, and claim their fulfillment, not because you are worthy, but because Christ has died for you. Plead the merits of his blood and take the Lord at his word.

Signs of the Times, March 9, 1888

What is the need?

_____
- -
- -
- -
- -

Praying for:

- ☐ Self
- ☐ Family
- ☐ Friend
- ☐ Church
- ☐ Ministry
- ☐ Life Issues

Bible Promise
See Promises to Claim pages: 121-133

_____
- -
- -
- -
- -
- -
- -
- -

Write your prayer using the Bible promise. Claim it again & again!
Invite the Holy Spirit to guide you as you write out your prayer.

Date:

Request Updates / Answer

Date:

Date:

Date:

The promises of God are not yea and nay, but yea and amen in Christ. If we would importune God, laying before him our needs in simplicity, with unfaltering confidence, in the name of Christ, we should receive of the abundance of the blessing of God. Tell the Lord exactly what you want in the way of spiritual blessings; and you need not fear to lay before him your temporal needs and perplexities. He has said..."Him that cometh to me I will in nowise cast out."

Signs of the Times, April 25, 1892

What is the need?

_____
_____
_____
_____

Bible Promise
See Promises to Claim pages: 121-133

_____
_____
_____
_____
_____
_____
_____
_____

Praying for:

☐ Self   ☐ Church

☐ Family   ☐ Ministry

☐ Friend   ☐ Life Issues

Write your prayer using the Bible promise. Claim it again & again!
Invite the Holy Spirit to guide you as you write out your prayer.

_____
_____
_____
_____
_____
_____
_____
_____
_____

Date:

Request Updates / Answer

Date: _____

Date: _____

Date: _____

Believe in the precious promises. Go to Jesus in childlike simplicity, and say, "Lord, I have borne these burdens as long as I can, and now I lay them upon the Burden-bearer." Do not gather them up again, but leave them all with Jesus. Go away free, for Jesus has set you free. He said, "I will give you rest." Take him at his word.

The Review and Herald, September 16, 1890

What is the need?

_____
_____
_____
_____

Bible Promise

See Promises to Claim pages: 121-133

_____
_____
_____
_____
_____
_____
_____

Praying for:

☐ Self   ☐ Church

☐ Family   ☐ Ministry

☐ Friend   ☐ Life Issues

Write your prayer using the Bible promise. Claim it again & again!

Invite the Holy Spirit to guide you as you write out your prayer.

_____
_____
_____
_____
_____
_____
_____
_____
_____

Date:

Request Updates / Answer

Date: _____

Date: _____

Date:

As laborers together with God, we should never neglect the precious privilege of prayer. The promise is given us, "Ask, and it shall be given you; seek, and ye shall find; knock, and it shall be opened unto you. For every one that asketh receiveth; and he that seeketh findeth; and to him that knocketh it shall be opened." Let us present our petition for grace and counsel, and plead that light be given us, that we may understand the Word. Let us pray for wisdom, that we may know how to communicate that Word for the encouragement of others.

Australasian Union Conference Record,
October 14, 1907

What is the need?

_____
_____
_____
_____

Praying for:

☐ Self   ☐ Church

☐ Family   ☐ Ministry

☐ Friend   ☐ Life Issues

Bible Promise
See Promises to Claim pages: 121-133

_____
_____
_____
_____
_____
_____
_____

Write your prayer using the Bible promise. Claim it again & again!
Invite the Holy Spirit to guide you as you write out your prayer.

_____
_____
_____
_____
_____
_____
_____
_____
_____
_____

Date:

Request Updates / Answer

Date: _____

Date: _____

Date:

Let us rejoice in the love
of God. Let us praise him
who has made us such
royal promises. Let these
promises keep our hearts
in perfect peace.

— The Youth's Instructor, January 23, 1902

What is the need?

Bible Promise
See Promises to Claim pages: 121-133

Praying for:

- [ ] Self
- [ ] Family
- [ ] Friend
- [ ] Church
- [ ] Ministry
- [ ] Life Issues

Write your prayer using the Bible promise. Claim it again & again!
Invite the Holy Spirit to guide you as you write out your prayer.

Date:

Request Updates / Answer

Date:

Date:

Date:

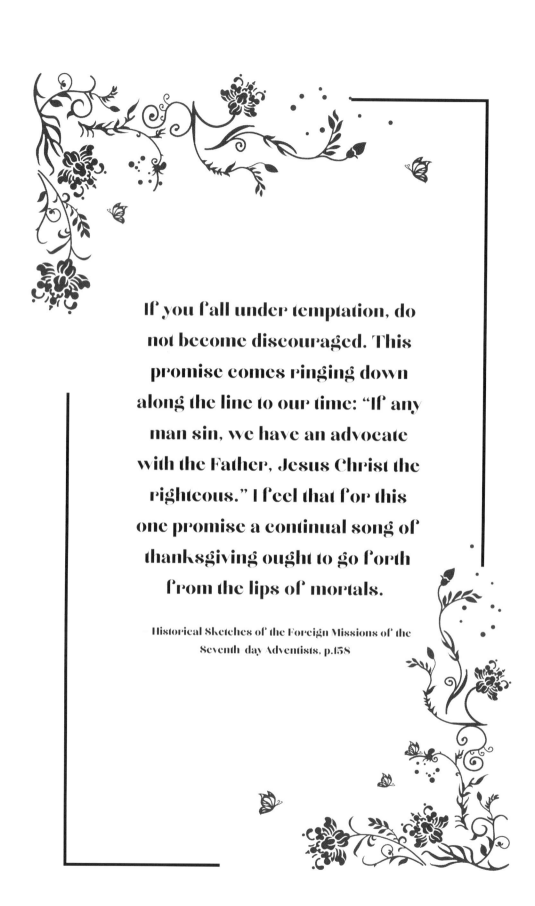

If you fall under temptation, do not become discouraged. This promise comes ringing down along the line to our time: "If any man sin, we have an advocate with the Father, Jesus Christ the righteous." I feel that for this one promise a continual song of thanksgiving ought to go forth from the lips of mortals.

Historical Sketches of the Foreign Missions of the Seventh-day Adventists, p.158

What is the need?

Bible Promise
See Promises to Claim pages: 121-133

Praying for:

☐ Self   ☐ Church
☐ Family   ☐ Ministry
☐ Friend   ☐ Life Issues

Write your prayer using the Bible promise. Claim it again & again!
Invite the Holy Spirit to guide you as you write out your prayer.

Date:

Request Updates / Answer

Date:

Date:

Date:

So with all the promises of God's word. In them He is speaking to us individually, speaking as directly as if we could listen to His voice. It is in these promises that Christ communicates to us His grace and power.

The Ministry of Healing, p.122

What is the need?

_____
_____
_____
_____

Praying for:

- ☐ Self
- ☐ Family
- ☐ Friend
- ☐ Church
- ☐ Ministry
- ☐ Life Issues

Bible Promise

See Promises to Claim pages: 121-133

_____
_____
_____
_____
_____
_____
_____
_____

Write your prayer using the Bible promise. Claim it again & again!

Invite the Holy Spirit to guide you as you write out your prayer.

_____
_____
_____
_____
_____
_____
_____
_____
_____
_____

Date:

Request Updates / Answer

Date: _____
Date: _____
Date: _____

When you do not feel the spirit of prayer, you should remember that feeling is not faith; you should seek to prove the pledged word of God. I have had to learn by experience that feeling is no criterion for us; we must take the word of God as the man of our counsel.

— Signs of the Times, December 15, 1890

What is the need?

Bible Promise
See Promises to Claim pages: 121-133

Praying for:

☐ Self   ☐ Church

☐ Family   ☐ Ministry

☐ Friend   ☐ Life Issues

Write your prayer using the Bible promise. Claim it again & again!
Invite the Holy Spirit to guide you as you write out your prayer.

Date:

Request Updates / Answer

Date:

Date:

Date:

"According to your faith be it unto you." "All things, whatsoever ye shall ask in prayer, believing, ye shall receive." Matthew 9:29; 21:22. Pray, believe, rejoice. Sing praises to God because He has answered your prayers. Take Him at His word. "He is faithful that promised." Hebrews 10:23.

Testimonies for the Church Volume 7, p.274

What is the need?

Bible Promise
See Promises to Claim pages: 121-133

Praying for:

- ☐ Self
- ☐ Family
- ☐ Friend
- ☐ Church
- ☐ Ministry
- ☐ Life Issues

Write your prayer using the Bible promise. Claim it again & again!
Invite the Holy Spirit to guide you as you write out your prayer.

Date:

Request Updates / Answer

Date:

Date:

Date:

It is not enough to say, "I believe;" we must exercise the living faith that claims the promises of God as our own, knowing that they are sure and steadfast... God is waiting to do great things for us as soon as we come into a right relation with him.

—Signs of the Times, November 11, 1889

What is the need?

Bible Promise
See Promises to Claim pages: 121-133

Praying for:

- ☐ Self
- ☐ Family
- ☐ Friend
- ☐ Church
- ☐ Ministry
- ☐ Life Issues

Write your prayer using the Bible promise. Claim it again & again!
Invite the Holy Spirit to guide you as you write out your prayer.

Date:

Request Updates / Answer

Date:

Date:

Date:

Many talk of faith, but it is only a lifeless faith. You must have faith that will claim Jesus as your Saviour today, that rests in the promises of God because they are the promises of God. You must be able to plant your feet on the eternal Rock, on the word of the great I AM.

The Review and Herald, March 4, 1890

What is the need?

_____
_____
_____
_____

Bible Promise

See Promises to Claim pages: 121-133

_____
_____
_____
_____
_____
_____
_____

Praying for:

☐ Self   ☐ Church
☐ Family   ☐ Ministry
☐ Friend   ☐ Life Issues

Write your prayer using the Bible promise. Claim it again & again!
Invite the Holy Spirit to guide you as you write out your prayer.

_____
_____
_____
_____
_____
_____
_____
_____
_____
_____

Date:

Request Updates / Answer

Date:
Date:
Date:

Do you plead with your children to come to Christ, and then go where there is no eye to see and no ear to hear, and there pour out your petitions before God for them?... We want the living faith that will grasp the strong arm of Jehovah. Christ said: "Ask, and it shall be given you; seek, and ye shall find; knock, and it shall be opened unto you." Here is the promise. Where is the faith to grasp the promise of God, and never give up until every child is gathered into the ark?

The Review and Herald, December 21, 1886

What is the need?

Bible Promise
See Promises to Claim pages: 121-133

Praying for:

- ☐ Self
- ☐ Family
- ☐ Friend
- ☐ Church
- ☐ Ministry
- ☐ Life Issues

Write your prayer using the Bible promise. Claim it again & again!
Invite the Holy Spirit to guide you as you write out your prayer.

Date:

Request Updates / Answer

Date:

Date:

Date:

Let us study the word of God
that we may know how to
take hold of His promises,
and claim them as our own.
Then we shall be happy.
The enemy will be unable
to destroy our peace.

Appeals for Unity, p.11

What is the need?

Bible Promise
See Promises to Claim pages: 121-133

Praying for:

☐ Self   ☐ Church
☐ Family   ☐ Ministry
☐ Friend   ☐ Life Issues

Write your prayer using the Bible promise. Claim it again & again!
Invite the Holy Spirit to guide you as you write out your prayer.

Date:

Request Updates / Answer

Date:

Date:

Date:

Cling to promises, with full faith in the One back of the promise. My brethren, have faith in a living all pitiful, and loving Saviour. "Fear thou not; for I am with thee: be not dismayed; for I am thy God: I will strengthen thee; yea, I will keep thee; yea I will uphold thee with the right hand of my righteousness." Your business now is simply to trust in the Lord.

Testimonies Relating to Emmanuel Missionary College and Its Work, p.7

What is the need?

Bible Promise
See Promises to Claim pages: 121-133

Praying for:

- [ ] Self
- [ ] Family
- [ ] Friend
- [ ] Church
- [ ] Ministry
- [ ] Life Issues

Write your prayer using the Bible promise. Claim it again & again!
Invite the Holy Spirit to guide you as you write out your prayer.

Date:

Request Updates / Answer

Date:

Date:

Date:

We must hold fast the promises.
These are the pledged words of
Him who is truth and verity; and
these are our assurances. They
can be appropriated to ourselves
only by individual faith... God
loves the thankful heart, trusting
implicitly in His words of
promise, gathering comfort and
hope and peace from them.

The Review and Herald, April 12, 1887

What is the need?

Bible Promise
See Promises to Claim pages: 121-133

Praying for:

☐ Self   ☐ Church

☐ Family   ☐ Ministry

☐ Friend   ☐ Life Issues

Write your prayer using the Bible promise. Claim it again & again!
Invite the Holy Spirit to guide you as you write out your prayer.

Date:

Request Updates / Answer

Date:

Date:

Date:

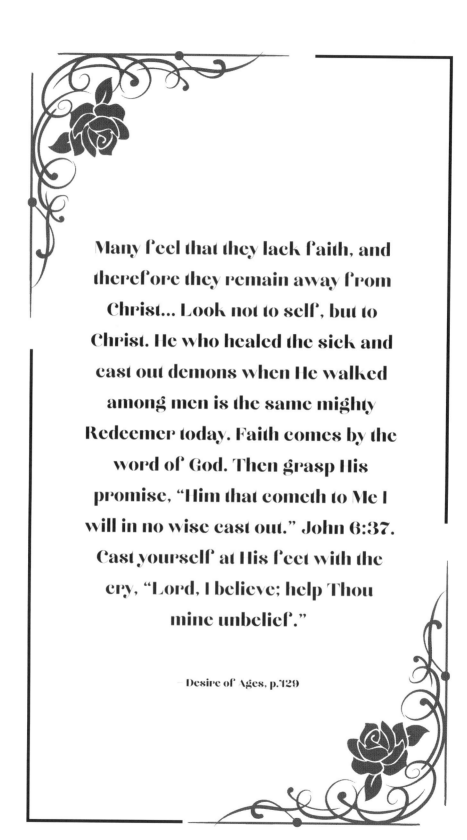

Many feel that they lack faith, and therefore they remain away from Christ... Look not to self, but to Christ. He who healed the sick and cast out demons when He walked among men is the same mighty Redeemer today. Faith comes by the word of God. Then grasp His promise, "Him that cometh to Me I will in no wise cast out." John 6:37. Cast yourself at His feet with the cry, "Lord, I believe; help Thou mine unbelief."

— Desire of Ages, p.429

What is the need?

Bible Promise
See Promises to Claim pages: 121-133

Praying for:

- ☐ Self
- ☐ Family
- ☐ Friend
- ☐ Church
- ☐ Ministry
- ☐ Life Issues

Write your prayer using the Bible promise. Claim it again & again!
Invite the Holy Spirit to guide you as you write out your prayer.

Date:

Request Updates / Answer

Date:

Date:

Date:

Trust in the Lord with all your heart, and
lean not on your own understanding; in
all your ways acknowledge Him, and He
will make your paths straight.

Proverbs 3:5,6

Promises to Claim

God's Word is rich with countless promises that offer strength, guidance, and assurance for every area of life. This quick reference guide is designed to help you easily access some of these promises. For a more in-depth collection, consider exploring one of the many books that organize these promises by topic.

Bible quotations are taken from the Berean Standard Bible unless otherwise noted.

And this is the confidence that we have before Him: If we ask anything according to His will, He hears us. And if we know that He hears us in whatever we ask, we know that we already possess what we have asked of Him.

— 1 John 5:14-15

Promises to Claim for
SELF

Who can discern his own errors? Cleanse me from my hidden faults. May the words of my mouth and the meditation of my heart be pleasing in Your sight, O Lord, my Rock and my Redeemer. — Psalm 19:12,14

Show me Your ways, O Lord; teach me Your paths. Guide me in Your truth and teach me, for You are the God of my salvation; all day long I wait for You. — Psalm 25:4,5

For day and night Your hand was heavy upon me; my strength was drained as in the summer heat. Then I acknowledged my sin to You and did not hide my iniquity. I said, "I will confess my transgressions to the Lord," and You forgave the guilt of my sin. — Psalm 32:4,5

I sought the Lord, and He answered me; He delivered me from all my fears. Those who look to Him are radiant with joy; their faces shall never be ashamed. — Psalm 34:4,5

If I had cherished iniquity in my heart, the Lord would not have listened. But God has surely heard; He has attended to the sound of my prayer. Blessed be God, who has not rejected my prayer or withheld from me His loving devotion! — Psalm 66:18-20

If I say, "My foot is slipping," Your loving devotion, O Lord, supports me. When anxiety overwhelms me, Your consolation delights my soul. — Psalm 94:18,19

The Lord is on my side; I will not be afraid. What can man do to me? It is better to take refuge in the Lord than to trust in man. — Psalm 118:6,8

Therefore I tell you, whatever you ask for in prayer, believe that you have received it, and it will be yours. And when you stand to pray, if you hold anything against another, forgive it, so that your Father in heaven will forgive your trespasses as well." — Mark 11:24,25

Then Jesus said to all of them, "If anyone wants to come after Me, he must deny himself and take up his cross daily and follow Me. If anyone is ashamed of Me and My words, the Son of Man will be ashamed of him when He comes in His glory...." — Luke 9:23,26

Promises to Claim for
SELF

Remain in Me, and I will remain in you. Just as no branch can bear fruit by itself unless it remains in the vine, neither can you bear fruit unless you remain in Me. If you remain in Me and My words remain in you, ask whatever you wish, and it will be done for you.   — John 15:4,7

For though we live in the flesh, we do not wage war according to the flesh. The weapons of our warfare are not the weapons of the world. Instead, they have divine power to demolish strongholds. We tear down arguments and every presumption set up against the knowledge of God; and we take captive every thought to make it obedient to Christ.   — 2 Corinthians 10:3-5

Surely you heard of Him and were taught in Him—in keeping with the truth that is in Jesus— to put off your former way of life, your old self, which is being corrupted by its deceitful desires; to be renewed in the spirit of your minds; and to put on the new self, created to be like God in true righteousness and holiness.   — Ephesians 4:21-24

Being confident of this, that He who began a good work in you will carry it on to completion until the day of Christ Jesus.   — Philippians 1:6

For it is God who works in you to will and to act on behalf of His good purpose. Do everything without complaining or arguing, so that you may be blameless and pure, children of God without fault in a crooked and perverse generation, in which you shine as lights in the world.   — Philippians 2:13-15

Set your minds on things above, not on earthly things. For you died, and your life is now hidden with Christ in God.   — Colossians 3:2,3

But when the kindness of God our Savior and His love for mankind appeared, He saved us, not by the righteous deeds we had done, but according to His mercy, through the washing of new birth and renewal by the Holy Spirit.
                           — Titus 3:4,5

Now may the God of peace...equip you with every good thing to do His will. And may He accomplish in us what is pleasing in His sight through Jesus Christ, to whom be glory forever and ever. Amen.   — Hebrews 13:20,21

Promises to Claim for
FAMILY

The Lord your God will circumcise your hearts and the hearts of your descendants, and you will love Him with all your heart and with all your soul, so that you may live.   — Deuteronomy 30:6

O God, You have taught me from my youth, and to this day I proclaim Your marvelous deeds. Even when I am old and gray, do not forsake me, O God, until I proclaim Your power to the next generation, Your might to all who are to come.   — Psalm 71:17,18

Give ear, O my people, to my instruction; listen to the words of my mouth. We will not hide them from their children, but will declare to the next generation the praises of the Lord and His might, and the wonders He has performed, that they should put their confidence in God, not forgetting His works, but keeping His commandments.   — Psalm 78:1,4,7

Before I was afflicted I went astray, but now I keep Your word. You are good, and do good; Teach me Your statutes.   — Psalm 119:67,68

One generation shall praise Your works to another, and shall declare Your mighty acts. Men shall speak of the might of Your awesome acts, And I will declare Your greatness.   — Psalm 145:4,6, NKJV

I will bring the blind by a way they did not know; I will lead them in paths they have not known. I will make darkness light before them, and crooked places straight. These things I will do for them, and not forsake them.   — Isaiah 42:16, NKJV

But thus says the Lord: "Even the captives of the mighty shall be taken away, and the prey of the terrible be delivered; For I will contend with him who contends with you, and I will save your children.   — Isaiah 49:25, NKJV

All your children shall be taught by the Lord, and great shall be the peace of your children..   — Isaiah 54:13, NKJV

"As for Me, this is My covenant with them," says the Lord. "My Spirit will not depart from you, and My words that I have put in your mouth will not depart from your mouth or from the mouths of your children and grandchildren, from now on and forevermore," says the Lord.   — Isaiah 59:21

Promises to Claim for
FAMILY

For I know the plans I have for you, declares the Lord, plans to prosper you and not to harm you, to give you a future and a hope.   — Jeremiah 29:11

I will give them one heart and one way, so that they will always fear Me for their own good and for the good of their children after them. I will make an everlasting covenant with them: I will never turn away from doing good to them, and I will put My fear in their hearts, so that they will never turn away from Me.   — Jeremiah 32:39,40

As a shepherd looks for his scattered sheep when he is among the flock, so I will look for My flock. I will rescue them from all the places to which they were scattered on a day of clouds and darkness. I will seek the lost, bring back the strays, bind up the broken, and strengthen the weak; but the sleek and strong I will destroy. I will shepherd them with justice.'   — Ezekiel 34:12,16

They will no longer defile themselves with their idols or detestable images, or with any of their transgressions. I will save them from all their apostasies by which they sinned, and I will cleanse them. Then they will be My people, and I will be their God.   — Ezekiel 37:23

But the Advocate, the Holy Spirit, whom the Father will send in My name, will teach you all things and will remind you of everything I have told you.
     — John 14:26

And Isaiah boldly says: "I was found by those who did not seek Me; I revealed Myself to those who did not ask for Me."   — Romans 10:20

He has rescued us from the dominion of darkness and brought us into the kingdom of His beloved Son, in whom we have redemption, the forgiveness of sins.   — Colossians 1:13,14

That they may be encouraged in heart, knit together in love, and filled with the full riches of complete understanding, so that they may know the mystery of God, namely Christ,   — Colossians 2:2

But the Lord is faithful, and He will strengthen you and guard you from the evil one. May the Lord direct your hearts into God's love and Christ's perseverance.   — 2 Thessalonians 3:3,5

Promises to Claim for
FRIENDS

For surely You, O Lord, bless the righteous; You surround them with the shield of Your favor.
— Psalm 5:12

Because he has set his love upon Me, therefore I will deliver him; I will set him on high, because he has known My name. He shall call upon Me, and I will answer him; I will be with him in trouble; I will deliver him and honor him.
— Psalm 91:14,15

The eyes of all look expectantly to You, and You give them their food in due season. You open Your hand and satisfy the desire of every living thing. The Lord is righteous in all His ways, gracious in all His works.
— Psalm 145:15-17

Anxiety weighs down the heart of a man, but a good word cheers it up.
— Proverbs 12:25

A man who has friends must himself be friendly, but there is a friend who sticks closer than a brother.
— Proverbs 18:24, NKJV

I will give them a heart to know Me, that I am the Lord. They will be My people, and I will be their God, for they will return to Me with all their heart.
— Jeremiah 24:7

I will give them one heart and one way, so that they will always fear Me for their own good and for the good of their children after them. I will make an everlasting covenant with them: I will never turn away from doing good to them, and I will put My fear in their hearts, so that they will never turn away from Me.
— Jeremiah 32:39,40

And I will give them singleness of heart and put a new spirit within them; I will remove their heart of stone and give them a heart of flesh, so that they may follow My statutes, keep My ordinances, and practice them. Then they will be My people, and I will be their God.
— Ezekiel 11:19,20

I will also sprinkle clean water on you, and you will be clean. I will cleanse you from all your impurities and all your idols. I will give you a new heart and put a new spirit within you; I will remove your heart of stone and give you a heart of flesh. And I will put My Spirit within you and cause you to walk in My statutes and to carefully observe My ordinances.
— Ezekiel 36:25-27

Promises to Claim for
FRIENDS

I ask that out of the riches of His glory He may strengthen you with power through His Spirit in your inner being, so that Christ may dwell in your hearts through faith. Then you, being rooted and grounded in love, will have power, together with all the saints, to comprehend the length and width and height and depth of the love of Christ, and to know this love that surpasses knowledge, that you may be filled with all the fullness of God.
— Ephesians 3:16-19

And this is my prayer: that your love may abound more and more in knowledge and depth of insight, so that you may be able to test and prove what is best and may be pure and blameless for the day of Christ, filled with the fruit of righteousness that comes through Jesus Christ, to the glory and praise of God.
— Philippians 1:9-11

That you may walk in a manner worthy of the Lord and may please Him in every way: bearing fruit in every good work, growing in the knowledge of God, being strengthened with all power according to His glorious might so that you may have full endurance and patience, and joyfully 1giving thanks to the Father, who has qualified you to share in the inheritance of the saints in the light.
— Colossians 1:10-12

Now may the God of peace Himself sanctify you completely, and may your entire spirit, soul, and body be kept blameless at the coming of our Lord Jesus Christ. The One who calls you is faithful, and He will do it. Brothers, pray for us as well.
— 1 Thessalonians 5:23-25

Therefore, brothers, stand firm and cling to the traditions we taught you, whether by speech or by letter. Now may our Lord Jesus Christ Himself and God our Father, who by grace has loved us and given us eternal comfort and good hope, encourage your hearts and strengthen you in every good word and deed.
— 2 Thessalonians 2:15-17

But the Lord is faithful, and He will strengthen you and guard you from the evil one. May the Lord direct your hearts into God's love and Christ's perseverance.
— 2 Thessalonians 3:3,5

The Lord will rescue me from every evil action and bring me safely into His heavenly kingdom. To Him be the glory forever and ever. Amen.
— 2 Timothy 4:18

Promises to Claim for
CHURCH

Do not turn aside after worthless things that cannot profit you or deliver you, for they are empty. Indeed, for the sake of His great name, the Lord will not abandon His people, because He was pleased to make you His own. As for me, far be it from me that I should sin against the Lord by ceasing to pray for you. And I will continue to teach you the good and right way.

— 1 Samuel 12:21-23

Know that the Lord is God. It is He who made us, and we are His; we are His people, and the sheep of His pasture. Enter His gates with thanksgiving and His courts with praise; give thanks to Him and bless His name.

— Psalm 100:3,4

Arise, shine, for your light has come, and the glory of the Lord rises upon you. For behold, darkness covers the earth, and thick darkness is over the peoples; but the Lord will rise upon you, and His glory will appear over you. Nations will come to your light, and kings to the brightness of your dawn. Lift up your eyes and look around: They all gather and come to you; your sons will come from afar, and your daughters will be carried on the arm.   — Isaiah 60:1-4

I will give them singleness of heart and put a new spirit within them; I will remove their heart of stone and give them a heart of flesh, so that they may follow My statutes, keep My ordinances, and practice them. Then they will be My people, and I will be their God.   — Ezekiel 11:19,20

At that time those who feared the Lord spoke with one another, and the Lord listened and heard them. So a scroll of remembrance was written before Him regarding those who feared the Lord and honored His name. "They will be Mine," says the Lord of Hosts, "on the day when I prepare My treasured possession. And I will spare them as a man spares his own son who serves him.   — Malachi 3:16,17

Again, I tell you truly that if two of you on the earth agree about anything you ask for, it will be done for you by My Father in heaven. For where two or three gather together in My name, there am I with them."   — Matthew 18:19,20

Promises to Claim for
CHURCH

You did not choose Me, but I chose you. And I appointed you to go and bear fruit—fruit that will remain—so that whatever you ask the Father in My name, He will give you.   — John 15:16

Again Jesus said to them, "Peace be with you. As the Father has sent Me, so also I am sending you." When He had said this, He breathed on them and said, "Receive the Holy Spirit.   — John 20:21,22

And hope does not disappoint us, because God has poured out His love into our hearts through the Holy Spirit, whom He has given us.   — Romans 5:5

Therefore let us pursue the things which make for peace and the things by which one may edify another.   — Romans 14:19

Now may the God who gives endurance and encouragement grant you harmony with one another in Christ Jesus, so that with one mind and one voice you may glorify the God and Father of our Lord Jesus Christ. Accept one another, then, just as Christ accepted you, in order to bring glory to God.   — Romans 15:5-7

We do not proclaim ourselves, but Jesus Christ as Lord, and ourselves as your servants for Jesus' sake. For God, who said, "Let light shine out of darkness," made His light shine in our hearts to give us the light of the knowledge of the glory of God in the face of Jesus Christ.   — 2 Corinthians 4:5,6

To this end, we always pray for you, that our God will count you worthy of His calling, and that He will powerfully fulfill your every good desire and work of faith, so that the name of our Lord Jesus will be glorified in you, and you in Him, according to the grace of our God and of the Lord Jesus Christ.   — 2 Thessalonians 1:11,12

Let us hold resolutely to the hope we profess, for He who promised is faithful. And let us consider how to spur one another on to love and good deeds. Let us not neglect meeting together, as some have made a habit, but let us encourage one another, and all the more as you see the Day approaching.   — Hebrews 10:23-25

But you are a chosen people, a royal priesthood, a holy nation, a people for God's own possession, to proclaim the virtues of Him who called you out of darkness into His marvelous light.   —1 Peter 2:9,10

Promises to Claim for
CHURCH MINISTRY

"Please, Lord," Moses replied, "I have never been eloquent, neither in the past nor since You have spoken to Your servant, for I am slow of speech and tongue." And the Lord said to him, "Who gave man his mouth?... Is it not I, the Lord? Now go! I will help you as you speak, and I will teach you what to say." — Exodus 4:10-12

The Lord Himself goes before you; He will be with you. He will never leave you nor forsake you. Do not be afraid or discouraged. — Deuteronomy 31:8

And Jabez called on the God of Israel saying, "Oh, that You would bless me indeed, and enlarge my territory, that Your hand would be with me, and that You would keep me from evil, that I may not cause pain!" So God granted him what he requested. — 1 Chronicles 4:10, NKJV

May God be gracious to us and bless us, and cause His face to shine upon us, that Your ways may be known on earth, Your salvation among all nations. Let the peoples praise You, O God; Let all the peoples praise You. — Psalm 67:1-3

The Lord God has given Me the tongue of the learned, that I should know how to speak a word in season to him who is weary. He awakens Me morning by morning, He awakens My ear to hear as the learned. — Isaiah 50:4, NKJV

My word that proceeds from My mouth will not return to Me empty, but it will accomplish what I please, and it will prosper where I send it. — Isaiah 55:11

Do not be afraid of them, for I am with you to deliver you," declares the Lord. Then the Lord reached out His hand, touched my mouth, and said to me: "Behold, I have put My words in your mouth." — Jeremiah 1:8,9

As you go, preach this message: "The kingdom of heaven is near." Heal the sick, raise the dead, cleanse the lepers, drive out demons. Freely you have received; freely give. — Matthew 10:7,8

Then Jesus came to them and said, "All authority in heaven and on earth has been given to Me. Therefore go and make disciples of all nations, baptizing them...and teaching them to obey all that I have commanded you. And surely I am with you always, even to the end of the age." — Matthew 28:18-20

Promises to Claim for
CHURCH MINISTRY

Then Jesus called the Twelve to Him and began to send them out two by two, giving them authority over unclean spirits. So they set out and preached that the people should repent. They also drove out many demons and healed many of the sick, anointing them with oil. — Mark 6:7,12,13

[God] comforts us in all our troubles, so that we can comfort those in any trouble with the comfort we ourselves have received from God. For just as the sufferings of Christ overflow to us, so also through Christ our comfort overflows. — 2 Corinthians 1:4,5

God was reconciling the world to Himself in Christ, not counting men's trespasses against them. And He has committed to us the message of reconciliation. Therefore we are ambassadors for Christ, as though God were making His appeal through us. We implore you on behalf of Christ: Be reconciled to God. — 2 Corinthians 5:19,20

Let us not grow weary in well-doing, for in due time we will reap a harvest if we do not give up. Therefore, as we have opportunity, let us do good to everyone, and especially to the family of faith. — Galatians 6:9,10

For it is God who works in you to will and to act on behalf of His good purpose, so that you may be blameless and pure, children of God without fault in a crooked and perverse generation, in which you shine as lights in the world as you hold forth the word of life.... — Philippians 2:13,15,16

Devote yourselves to prayer, being watchful and thankful, as you pray also for us, that God may open to us a door for the word, so that we may proclaim the mystery of Christ, for which I am in chains. Pray that I may declare it clearly, as I should. — Colossians 4:2-4

The prayer offered in faith will restore the one who is sick. The Lord will raise him up. If he has sinned, he will be forgiven. Therefore confess your sins to each other and pray for each other so that you may be healed. The prayer of a righteous man has great power to prevail. — James 5:15.16

If anyone speaks, he should speak as one conveying the words of God. If anyone serves, he should serve with the strength God provides, so that in all things God may be glorified through Jesus Christ, to whom be the glory and the power forever and ever. Amen. — 1 Peter 4:11

Promises to Claim for
LIFE ISSUES

The Lord will fight for you; you need only to be still.   — Exodus 14:14

Yet the Lord your God would not listen to Balaam, and the Lord your God turned the curse into a blessing for you, because the Lord your God loves you.
— Deuteronomy 23:5

This Book of the Law must not depart from your mouth; meditate on it day and night, so that you may be careful to do everything written in it. For then you will prosper and succeed in all you do. Have I not commanded you to be strong and courageous? Do not be afraid; do not be discouraged, for the Lord your God is with you wherever you go.   — Joshua 1:8,9

Perhaps the Lord will see my affliction and repay me with good for the cursing I receive today.   — 2 Samuel 16:12

Then Asa cried out to the Lord his God: "O Lord, there is no one besides You to help the powerless against the mighty. Help us, O Lord our God, for we rely on You, and in Your name we have come against this multitude. O Lord, You are our God. Do not let a mere mortal prevail against You."
— 2 Chronicles 14:11

I will lie down and sleep in peace, for You alone, O Lord, make me dwell in safety.   — Psalm 4:8

The righteous cry out, and the Lord hears; He delivers them from all their troubles. The Lord is near to the brokenhearted; He saves the contrite in spirit. Many are the afflictions of the righteous, but the Lord delivers him from them all.   — Psalm 34:17-19

I once was young and now am old, yet never have I seen the righteous abandoned or their children begging for bread.   — Psalm 37:25

Call upon Me in the day of trouble; I will deliver you, and you will honor Me.
— Psalm 50:15

The Lord is on my side; I will not be afraid. What can man do to me? It is better to take refuge in the Lord than to trust in man.   — Psalm 118:6,8

Promises to Claim for
LIFE ISSUES

Do not fear, for I am with you; do not be afraid, for I am your God. I will strengthen you; I will surely help you; I will uphold you with My right hand of righteousness.   — Isaiah 41:10

For this is what the Lord says: "Your injury is incurable; your wound is grievous. But I will restore your health and heal your wounds, declares the Lord..."   — Jeremiah 30:12,17

"... if You can do anything, have compassion on us and help us." "If You can?" echoed Jesus. "All things are possible to him who believes!" Immediately the boy's father cried out, "I do believe; help my unbelief!"   — Mark 9:22-24

For our light and momentary affliction is producing for us an eternal weight of glory that is far beyond comparison. So we fix our eyes not on what is seen, but on what is unseen. For what is seen is temporary, but what is unseen is eternal.   — 2 Corinthians 4:17,18

I can do all things through Christ who gives me strength.   — Philippians 4:13

And my God will supply all your needs according to His glorious riches in Christ Jesus.   — Philippians 4:19

Make sure that no one repays evil for evil. Always pursue what is good for one another and for all people. Rejoice at all times. Pray without ceasing. Give thanks in every circumstance, for this is God's will for you in Christ Jesus.
                                                        — 1 Thessalonians 5:15-18

So do not throw away your confidence; it holds a great reward. You need to persevere, so that after you have done the will of God, you will receive what He has promised.   — Hebrews 10:35,36

Our fathers disciplined us for a short time as they thought best, but God disciplines us for our good, so that we may share in His holiness. No discipline seems enjoyable at the time, but painful. Later on, however, it yields a harvest of righteousness and peace to those who have been trained by it.
                                                        — Hebrews 12:10,11

Do not repay evil with evil or insult with insult, but with blessing, because to this you were called so that you may inherit a blessing.   — 1 Peter 3:9

Be anxious for nothing, but in everything, by prayer and petition, with thanksgiving, present your requests to God. And the peace of God, which surpasses all understanding, will guard your hearts and your minds in Christ Jesus.

Philippians 4:6,7

Favorite Bible Promises

Use this section to write down Bible promises that are meaningful to you. As you study the Scriptures, find verses that speak to your heart and circumstances. You may also consider exploring books on prayer promises to find additional inspiration.

In every command and in every promise of the word of God is the power, the very life of God, by which the command may be fulfilled and the promise realized. He who by faith receives the word is receiving the very life and character of God.

Christ's Object Lessons, p.38

Favorite Bible Promises

Search the Scriptures and write down other promises that speak to your heart

---

Not one of all the Lord's good promises to the house of Israel
had failed; everything was fulfilled. — Joshua 21:45

Favorite Bible Promises

Search the Scriptures and write down other promises that speak to your heart

_____

_____

_____

_____

_____

_____

_____

_____

_____

_____

_____

_____

_____

_____

_____

_____

_____

_____

_____

Yet he did not waver through disbelief in the promise of God, but was strengthened in his faith and gave glory to God, being fully persuaded that God was able to do what He had promised.. — Romans 4:20,21

Favorite Bible Promises

Search the Scriptures and write down other promises that speak to your heart

_____
_____
_____
_____
_____
_____
_____
_____
_____
_____
_____
_____
_____
_____
_____
_____
_____
_____
_____
_____
_____
_____
_____

What then shall we say in response to these things? If God is for us, who can be against us? He who did not spare His own Son but gave Him up for us all, how will He not also, along with Him, freely give us all things? — Romans 8:31,32

Favorite Bible Promises

Search the Scriptures and write down other promises that speak to your heart

_____

_____

_____

_____

_____

_____

_____

_____

_____

_____

_____

_____

_____

_____

_____

_____

_____

_____

_____

_____

_____

_____

For all the promises of God are "Yes" in Christ. And so through Him,
our "Amen" is spoken to the glory of God. — 2 Corinthians 1:20

Favorite Bible Promises

Search the Scriptures and write down other promises that speak to your heart

Let us hold resolutely to the hope we profess, for He
who promised is faithful. — Hebrews 10:23

Made in the USA
Columbia, SC
13 May 2025

57867730R00078